Desolate Dream

Desolate Dream

Laura Margiotta Grenier

To order additional copies of this book, contact:
Xlibris Corporation
1-888-795-4274
www.Xlibris.com
Orders@Xlibris.com
34091

CONTENTS

Dedication

To my children
Danielle, Anthony, Zachary
The best and dearest gifts of my life-
With all my heart and love

My Mother

She enhanced my life . . .
And because of her, I am a more loving, compassionate, and understanding person.
She taught me to see the best in myself and others.
To reveal that best with integrity that could not be denied.
Like a shining star, she had an inner light that shone out and made my days brighter.
Nothing in life . . . will ever make up for the kind of mother I have lost.

"A Poet...
Is someone who can pour light into a cup
And then raise it to nourish your
Beautiful—
Perhaps parched—holy mouth"

—Hafiz

Desolate Dream

I keep holding on . . .
Waiting to exhale . . .
The pain that succumbs my inner being
The Poetry of my soul . . .
In the form of a blank verse . . .
I keep holding on . . .
Waiting . . . .
For your love to encumber me . . .
Like a desolate dream.

" . . . And when we grow old, I will find two chairs and set them close each sun-lit
day . . . that you and I . . . in quiet joy . . . may rock the world away . . ."
Unknown Author

Life

Feeling bereft as my daughter left for college . . .
I wanted to keep things as it was . . .
Because . . . soon afterwards . . . graduation . . .
Marriage . . .
She would become someone . . .
A woman . . . someone's wife . . . a mother . . .
I just wanted her to always be my baby . . .
The depth and potency of a relationship between a mother and a daughter . . .
Mythical . . .
The joys and agony of having a daughter . . .
And LETTING HER GO . . .
Watching her become her own person . . .
Experiencing life on her own terms . . .
The juices are flowing . . .
Feeling alive . . .
The vitality I see in her . . .
In my child . . .
I WAS ONCE HER . . .
The powerful emotions . . .
A mother is the only person that can make a family nourish . . .
We all want to be a mother . . .
Who is fun and carefree . . .
Instead of a mother who has to be dealt with . . .
We are mainly a vessel . . .
Her journey is clearly her own . . .
We all have to let them go at some point . . .
Losing a daughter . . .
To the great seduction called
LIFE . . .

"Embrace integrity, honesty, loyalty and compassion . . . and develop values and
virtues. It's time to grow up . . . Life's out there awaiting"
Unknown Author

Untitled

I crave you . . .
I taste you . . .
Sweet as candy . . .
bitter as lemon.
You are my heartbreak . . .
You are my sadness . . .
You are my happiness . . .
You are my madness.
It is you I crave . . .
Behind those sad eyes.
Sweet as candy . . .
Bitter as lemon.

Let me go

You're pushing me away . . .
Your heart so hard to find.
As you hide behind your eyes full of melancholy . . .
As cold as ice . . .
Is there any warmth left within you . . .
Ritual taunting, which faded and flared
According to the moon and seasons . . .
As Time holds the key.
To the future.
My heart clouded . . .
Like the black of the blackest ocean . . .
The power you possess you will never know . . .
Yet . . .
There are pieces of me you have never seen.
Are we past the point of no return . . .
Side by side . . . we move, in sync no longer . . .
Further apart . . .
Is it Time . . .
For me to say . . . .
. . . Goodbye . . .

Loves Surround Me

Love surround me with all your reach . . .
I need your love and you beside me.
There is a place for us . . .
Somewhere . . .
A sunny afternoon autumn in the air . . .
Crisp and clear . . .
The leaves full of colors of the rainbow.
Hand in hand we walk . . .
In sync.
Somewhere the rhapsody of our souls
Reunite . . .
The passion that once was . . .
Love surround me with all your reach . . .

"Love . . . is the passionate dance between
Two hearts . . . It is to believe in the dream, and together make it real."
Sylvanna Rossetti

The Silent Voice

Your eyes have their silence . . .
I cannot bare.
The void with no sound.
Unleashing your soul
Only I can see.
Without ever saying a word.
Our souls reunite.
Sharing the same intimacies and feelings.
The truth is in the eyes . . .
The silent voice . . .

Tragic Eyes

Eyes as green as the sea . . .
Haunted and haunting
In these eyes
You can read the tragedy of a drained life.
Eyes that glare . . .
With utter coldness . . .
Lacking softness.
Eyes that challenge me . . .
They disturb . . .
Yet, I cannot turn away.

Fallen

I never promised you a ray of sunshine . . .
I only promised you my love . . .
I thought I found the one . . .
The one to spend eternity.
My soul mate.
Afraid of being hurt . . .
Afraid of being vulnerable.
Stay with me tonight . . .
One last encounter
Entwined like spoons . . .
Reminisce of our past.
I never promised you a ray of sunshine . . .
I only promised you my love . . .
Forgive me . . .
For the blue skies that have FALLEN GREY.

Another World

I love my husband . . .
But he is in another world . . .
And I too . . . Dream of another world.
Eager to learn . . .
Easy to please . . .
Help me unite . . .
I try to be patient and understand . . .
A stranger . . . really . . . to my own self . . .
Or any other soul.
Yet . . .
I do not want to be anonymous.
I want to count the stars . . .
On our path
Whatever the future holds . . .
Together . . .
As for now . . . I hide . . .
In my glass body . . .
Ready to shatter in a million little pieces.
I too . . . have appetites . . .
Fears . . .
Pain . . .
I don't have the luxury to think in terms of destiny.
I love my husband . . .
But he is in another world . . .
I too . . .
Dream . . .
Of ANOTHER WORLD . . .

"What lies behind us and what lies before us . . . are tiny matters
compared to what lies within us"
Unknown Author

Four Hands

It doesn't take two souls destined for one another
To make a good marriage.
It takes two individuals headed in the same direction.
The same path in life . . .
And to slow down once in awhile to let the other catch up.
Love is not just about flowers and candy kisses
It's about these four hands . . .
Together . . .
Created a life . . .
A world . . .
entwined like spoons . . .
Love is about someone who will always
Stand by your side . . .
EVEN . . .
If you're wrong.

"Nothing is more beautiful than the love that has weathered The storms of life"
Jerome K. Jerome

Alone

The house so mysteriously silent . . .
Listening . . .
Waiting . . .
For some conversation.
Instead . . .
Alone I would be . . .
Waiting silently . . .
Crying . . .
Hot tears . . . stayed trapped and burning
On my wounded soul . . .
Listening to the silence . . .
. . . . once again . . .
As another day begins . . .
Wondering . . .
What was worse???
Being lonely . . .
Or
Being alone . . . .

The Spinning Carousel

Many years ago . . .
I fell under your spell.
Like a spinning carousel.
Rising and falling . . .
rising and falling.
I breathed you in like oxygen . . .
Holding you there.
Never wanting to exhale.
I use to think no one else was above you.
The memories of you are like gold charms on a bracelet . . .
One by one . . .
You look back and you discover the beauty and sadness
Of the radical intimacy it represents.
Raindrops . . . as they fall on the rooftop
Gentle . . . like beautiful music . . .
Letting you forget . . .
The bureaucrats . . .
As you listen to the pitter patter of the rain.
Remembering . . . .
As I fell under the spell . . .
Of the spinning carousel.

The Familiar Stranger

You slam your manhood against these walls . . .
As you threaten our foundation.
This rage inside you becomes immense . . .
From a stir . . .
To a volcanic rupture.
It rattles sacred bones, that shatter like glass . . .
This mold once formed and once shaped . . .
By some magical will . . .
Now trapped and crushed in a severed cage.
My hatred for you grows . . .
As your music escalates much louder.
Yet . . . I understand . . .
The familiar stranger who has stepped into our lives.
The passion and laughter in your heart.
The hopes and dreams once bound us together . . .
Forever gone . . .
This ancient rhythm that wells in you . . .
My one true love . . .
The familiar stranger . . .
I cannot hold these walls up alone.
I NEED YOU . . .
To carry on.

Untitled

Highly cultured, and well spoken . . .
Audacious . . .
Rich and famous . . .
The peripatetic woman who has everything.
Remarkably independent . . .
Extravagant jewelry and wardrobe.
Dressing tables full of cosmetics and perfume.
The Independent female . . .
The possibility in our era . . .
To reach for the stars . . .
The successful woman . . .
In this life . . .
ANYTHING . . .
IS . . . .
POSSIBLE . . .

Untitled

Someday when I am old . . .
I will be rocking in my chair . . .
Overlooking the crystal sea.
I don't know if you will be there by my side with me . . .
many regrets . . .
many setbacks . . .
Searching for solace . . .
Never to be found.
Searching for security on solid ground.
Like glue, by your side, I have always been . . .
Too weak . . .
Insecure . . .
To let go . . .
Of the reigns you have on me.
We were wrong right from the start.
Hand in hand, you stole my heart.
Someday when I am old . . .
I will be rocking in my chair . . .
Overlooking the crystal sea . . .
MAYBE . . .
You will be there with me . . .

Life's Rewards

Sophistication . . .
Style . . .
Self assured . . .
A passionate appreciation for the finer things in life . . .
Champagne and caviar . . .
Jaguar and Mercedes Benz . . .
Fancy cars . . . mansions in Bel Aire . . .
A connoisseur of life's rewards.

Italy . . .

One gigantic museum . . .
Inspiring . . . yet . . . terrifying . . .
A journey across the Adriatic sea . . .
Through the clamorous markets of St. Petersburg Square . . .
The wondrous landscaping . . .
Like an empty canvas . . .
Waiting for a splash of color . . .
Emotions within lifted . . .
The poetry of your soul . . .
A dream that keeps returning . . .
. . . for the rest of your life . . . .

"To see the summer sky . . . is poetry"
Emily Dickinson

Sanctuary

All winter . . .
I envision the exquisite secret garden . . .
The beautiful blooms
I can even smell them.
{as wonderful as they use to smell in my mothers garden}
Fresh air . . .
The buzz of the bees around.
Sunshine on my shoulders . . .
Monarch butterflies dancing all about . . .
A dreamy feeling . . . here . . .
Quiet . . .
Introspective . . .
Serene . . .
Savoring the sights and scents . . .
Entranced by the beauty . . .
So close to nature . . .
At peace . . .
Alluring.

Time

The focus of time is an illusion . . .
Ticking away at the years.
An experience . . .
. . . not always good . . .
. . . sometimes bad
you deal with life's trials and tribulations
you manipulate them to your advantage . . . .
How capricious . . .
The eternal spark of life . . .

Imaginary World

A world where time isn't measured by alarms and deadlines.
Countless hours on the porch . . . .
Enjoying the autumn breeze.
The wonderful ambience of autumn.
A world where there is lush woodland and cranberry bogs.
Homes nestled among hilltops with breathtaking views.
A beautiful domain . . .
Where the lengthening of afternoon shadows . . .
Begin the rhythm of the season.
The natural splendor which invigorates and inspires.
The natural wonders of my imaginary world . . .
My heaven on earth . . .
Where time is measured by love and harmony.

The Winding road

Traveling down this old road . . .
Trying to find my way home . . .
Driving and driving . . .
In autopilot mode . . .
A decision to be made . . .
Weighing heavily on my mind.
The choices I must make . . .
Effecting my future . . .
What will the wise men say???
What will the crystal ball foresee . . .
What will my future be . . .
As I travel down this old road . . .
Follow my heart . . .
Or . . .
Follow my head . . .
Where do I start . . .
Where does it end . . .
Give me a sign so I can understand . . .
The rain is falling down on my window pane . . .
The music escalates . . .
As I hear the sound of the drums . . .
Pounding on my wounded soul . . .
Life is about living . . .
Not living in bondage . . .
Waiting for emotions to erupt like a volcano . . .
Traveling down this old road . . .
Trying to find my way home . . .
Where are the virtues we held so high??

Broken . . .
Frozen in time . . .
Shattered in a million pieces . . .
Who holds the key to my future??
What will the wise men say??
Love is letting go . . .
A lesson my soul has to learn . . .

"not I nor anyone else can travel that road for you. You must travel it yourself"
Walt Whitman

Snowbound

The snow how it blankets the street . . .
Making it almost mandatory to play . . .
Snowbound at home . . .
The unexpected snowstorm . . .
A chance to recover our childhoods sense of time.
A journey . . .
Before our over scheduled life . . . .
How now we appreciate the respite of the warmth of home . . .
Of a loving family . . .
A fire crackling . . .
Hot cocoa . . .
Cookies and cake
Fresh from the oven.
We dust off our childhood games . . .
Buried deep in the attic . . .
As we play a rousing game of monopoly . . .
No computers
No cell phones . . . xbox or play station . . .
A time to reconnect . . .
No cars can be heard . . .
Snowed in . . .
Snuggled within our family unit . . .
Relying on each other for amusement . . .
In the days of my childhood . . .
This is what my brother and I did every day . . .
A time that suddenly didn't seem so long ago . . .
As the snowstorm puts me back in touch with
What really matters in life . . .
The warmth of
A
Loving family . . .

Untitled

The initial shock . . .
Will there ever be happiness again???
Only bare essentials accomplished.
Breathing . . .
Beyond just existing.
The depth . . .
The scope of pain.
Unbearable . . .
Unimaginable . . .
Time . . . passes . . .
Life becomes manageable . . .
We learn to live . . .
The facts . . .
Continuously struggling to survive . . .
To come back home.

My Table

A place where you serve surprise . . .
Opinions . . .
Sometimes fact . . .
Arguments and great conversation . . .
A place to eat and a place for celebrations . . .
Our dinner table . . .
Where our family is connected . . .
A moment to converse . . .
Reconnect . . .

New York City

People in your face . . .
Fast paced . . . running . . .
Cabbies beeping at you . . .
Sirens going off . . .
High energy . . .
Like six espressos . . .
caffeine out . . .
Crowded spaces . . .
The green valley of central park . . .
Skyscrapers by the hundreds . . .
Dazzling architecture . . .
One of the most familiar skylines in the world . . .
The empire state building . . .
The statue of liberty . . .
Bloomingdale's . . .
Barney's . . .
The stock exchange . . .
MTV and Times Square . . .
Limos and celebrities . . .
The metropolitan life . . .
High energy . . .
The city that never sleeps . . .
New York . . .

Portent

Sitting on the beach one evening . . .
I see the crescent moon over the waters.
My mind starts to reminisce . . .
To a different time.
How a sequence of events have changed my
World.
What happened to the young, vivacious soul . . .
Carefree . . .
Full of life . . .
All that remains is a wounded soul . . .
Cold . . .
PORTENT . . .
Dying within . . .
Bare trees under white sky.

Solace

Feeling stagnant . . .
As fear at times, completely immobilized me.
Wasting so much effort . . .
Languishing on regret . . .
Always wondering . . .
What if . . .
Brave on the outside for the world to see . . .
Deep inside . . .
Living in bondage with emotions ready to erupt.
Life goes on . . .
No matter how difficult the road seems.
We need to find the key to open the door to
SOLACE . . .

Heaven's Door

The beating of the drums . . .
Are pounding on my wounded soul.
It's raining . . .
It's raining . . .
It's storming in my mind.
I think of all that was lost and all that was left behind.
It's raining . . .
It's raining . . .
It's storming in my mind.
I think back on all of life's sins.
It's turbulent winds . . . blowing wild in my mind . . .
There's no use hiding from the wings of life.
Say goodbye to what was then . . . the future is in Heaven's Door . . .
The inner core of life . . .
It's raining . . .
It's raining . . .
It's storming in my mind.

Maybe Tomorrow

The children how they waited for me to get home from work. Up at
five am . . . work . . . work . . . work. All those sacrifices so they could
have the wonderful things life has to offer. Private schools and camps.
Sports, music lessons, designer clothes. The velocity of our modern life.
I look at how they have grown . . . teenagers now . . . Driving cars and dating.
I remember waiting at the bus stop that first September day,
with knapsacks too heavy for their little backs to hurl.
The best of what the world has to offer at their fingertip. I worry . . .
that I have failed them . . . I was too busy . . . building a career.
Tasks so important, ultimately, they wash away like castles in the sand.
I can't remember a time . . . when I had TIME. To feel the leaves
crunching, to enjoy the sunset, to smell the roses,
to enjoy a spectacular view . . . my CHILDREN . . .
I remember when they use to ask me to read to them and to take them to the
park. Always too busy . . . Tomorrow . . . "after I finish this", when I have more
time, more energy. Always too busy, never enough time . . . for my children.
I've missed their childhood. These thoughts race through my mind as
they haunt my inner being. Have I failed to teach them the meaning of life,
by giving them everything money can buy . . . except . . . TIME. Time spent
together with the warmth of family. Years have past. Time, I now have for them.
Yet,the pages have turned . . . "No time mom, I'm too busy, too much to do . . .
maybe tomorrow". . . . yes . . . MAYBE TOMORROW.

My Precious Gift

She has changed my life and the meaning of it from the moment she arrived. The second I looked into those wandering, big, brown Eyes, as she lay, newly born on my chest. I saw it with clarity. "The miracle of life" I cherished her instantly. She was my top priority, my duty to love, guide, protect, and of course, enjoy rapturously and completely.

How I wish I were a perfect woman, that I may never fail her; but alas, at times I have. I've tried to teach her the value of hard work, good judgment, courage and honesty. I've tried to give her everything materialistic and to love her perfectly as she deserves to be. I will always try, until my last my breath, to give her that.

I am so grateful to have had a chance to love her, know her, teach and guide her, and appreciate her. To have passed on the gift of life that was given to me. What a miracle she is! I hope that these eighteen years I have done my best to prepare her for her own life's journey. I have learned daily from her. She has opened My eyes and solidified my understanding of this truth with her first breath. As she starts a new chapter in her life, she will face new challenges. She is a bright, beautiful, young woman that has blossomed right before my eyes. I will always be here for her, to celebrate her successes and accept her defeats as she starts her own life's journey. My Daughter . . . . My Miracle . . . . My Precious Gift.

Beautiful child

Where is my beautiful little boy . . .
The handsome child who brought me joy . . .
Like a ship lost in the ocean . . .
A world in commotion . . .
Mesmerized by your own inner beings . . .
Full of silence and full of inner rage you keep hidden deep inside . . .
You want to navigate the uncharted wilderness . . .
Yet . . .
Like a plane during a thunderstorm . . .
No visibility . . .
No direction . . .
Out of control . . .
Out of reach . . .

Zachary Jon

My little angel sent from up above . . .
You have brought me happiness . . .
And so much love . . .
I look into your eyes of gray . . .
I thank God every single day . . .
That you were sent for me to love . . .
My little angel . . .
From up above . . .

"The most beautiful things can't be seen or touched.
They are felt through the heart."
Linda Greyson

Untitled

One November day . . . autumn in the air . . .
A split second . . .
Life changes . . .
The slightest justification . . .
The world you planned . . .
Now . . . in turmoil
Adjusted plans . . .
Revised expectations . . .
Life goes on . . . it doesn't STOP . . .
Yet . . . we are wrestling with the reality of a life . . .
Turned upside down . . .
Did I do enough???
Understand enough???
To the world, we learned to show a normal face.
Living in a such a challenging world . . .
Stronger . . .
For observing his strength.
An experience which made our life more meaningful . . .
A revised perspective . . .
About what is important in LIFE . . .

Faces of strangers

Faces . . .
Expressions . . .
A room full of strong odors . . .
Some look two or three days past bathing.
Some . . . their clean scent . . . refreshes the area
Noone pays attention
As they look and stare into oblivion . . .
Eyes . . .
Different colors, shapes . . .
Some expressive, some distinctive . . .
Noises . . . sounds . . . smells . . . voices . . .
Everyone in tune to themselves.
Faces . . .
They come . . . they go . . .
First stop, second stop, and so forth . . .
never to see the same face again.
Such a vast world we live in . . .
This society . . . with so many faces . . .
Yet . . .
No one seems to smile
Or even gesture "hello"
Only stares . . . if your pretty or famous . . .
Then . . . and only then . . .
Everyone wants to be your friend
Even smiles, gestures of "hello".
Strangers all around . . .
All you see are the eyes protruding out of their seats.
Faces of strangers . . .
Strangers we encounter on our daily commute . . .
Never to encounter again.
Did you know that I am a mother . . .

A poet . . .

A kind soul . . .

No one knows who the stranger next to you is . . .

No one knows what they have gone through in their world . . .

Did you know I suffered loss . . . pain . . . . heartache too . . . .

I'm sure you didn't know . . .

Would you even care . . .

Don't judge a book by its cover.

An elderly gentleman, cane in hand . . .

Enters . . .

No seats available . . .

You could see the pain of life through his distinctive, caring eyes . . .

A kindred soul.

Yet . . .

No one gives up their seat . . .

Young and healthy . . .

The faces of strangers . . .

Selfish . . . unkind . . .

Our society . . . today . . .

The daily encounters of these faces of strangers.

Funny . . . how unsociable, uncaring, and

Judgmental we really are . . .

Try riding the train sometime . . .

You'll know what I mean . . .

Artistic Phenomenon

From Monet . . . to VanGogh . . .
Degas to Renoir . . .
A period of upheaval
The rebuilding of Paris . . .
The rise of industrialism . . .
Paintings . . .
Startlingly shocking . . .
Sensibility . . . urbane . . .
Contemporary . . .
Changing . . .
The loose coalition . . .
The beginning of an era . . .
Impressionism . . .
The nineteenth century phenomenon . . .
Still . . .
So appealing . . .
Mesmerizing . . .
In this day and age . . .

Music

Abstract and sublime of all arts . . .
How it moves our lives . . .
A universal,non verbal language . . .
It allows us to transcend into our own world . . .
And partake in utterly different realities . . .
Music . . .
A pseudoscience . . .
An adjectival palette by which we isolate . . .
Events that we may not even be able to notice . . .
Music . . .

Untitled

I stare down at my stagnant life . . .
As sensitive memories come flashing . . .
Melancholy evocations of lost love . . .
Love passes . . .
Yet . . .
Solitude persists . . .
Leaving me weary with few remnants . . .
Mere memories of which I have created.
Temporary solace . . .
My soul is bruised by my ego . . .
With disturbing memory.
How crucial . . .
Life changing moments pass through our hands . . .
. . . without ever knowing it.
Sometimes . . . two lonely trajectories . . .
Intersect . . .
Irrefutably . . .
Emotionally charged . . .
A distance between us . . .

Shattered Epiphany

My lessons have been hard and long.
As I blame everyone for my mistakes . . .
And all that has gone wrong.
I wish I had an epiphany through all this.
A vast canvas to paint however I choose.
Yet . . . vigorously through others I have lived.
With delusions of grandeur . . .
I want to stay suspended in a moment of time . . .
Putting off the inevitable.
My moves are the result of someone else's direction.
My world shattered into a million shards.
I have always danced to my own artistic beat . . .
Defying defeat . . .
Yet . . .
So much of life is fate.
It seems inconclusive . . .
We must treasure the cerulean skies . . .
Like they are precious gems . . .
Will we ever be prepared for the tumultuous
Seas of life on our own . . .
The sting of unpleasantness . . .
From failure . . . .

Shattered Dreams

The world thought you had it all . . .
Painterly perfectionism . . .
A vision of an ideal loving family . . .
A beautiful home . . .
Prestigious careers . . .
A financial dream . . .
An enchanting life.
You wanted to touch life . . .
Passion . . .
Beauty . . .
And creativity.
Instead . . .
You are at the edge of the ocean . . .
Just about to fall in.
The world thought you had it all.
No one knows what lies behind closed doors . . .
A secret interior life . . .
Hidden away in a closet . . .
As you put on a masquerade for the world to see.
Two loving souls . . .
Once intersected . . .
Now . . .
A distance between them exists.

Letting Go

Deep set dark and piercing eyes . . .
Buried in high cheekbones . . .
A smile that made you believe anything.
Remember . . .
How we use to dream . . .
About faraway places . . .
Entwined like spoons we slept . . .
Longing for each others warmth and touch.
Somehow . . .
We stopped loving and having conversations . . .
We got lost . . .
Becoming defensive and resentful . . .
You want to believe in forever . . .
Yet . . .
Time is limited . . .
You were letting me go easily . . .
Perhaps . . .
Because . . .
I had left along time ago . . .

Pieces of me

I blame everyone for my misery . . .
My passive aggressiveness has turned everyone I love away from me . . .
Yet . . .
You're still here by my side . . .
You have seen every part of me . . .
My laughter . . .
My smiles . . .
My dark side too . . .
Yet . . .
You're still by my side . . .
Hypocrisy . . .
Controversy . . .
Worlds to conquer . . .
my greatest enemy . . .
An unspoken despair kept hidden inside . . .
Never had the strength to go very far . . .
My voice at times weak and wavering . . .
Yet . . .
You're still by my side . . .
Searching for a sanctuary . . .
Where beauty lives . . .
Will my day come when I get my rainbow?
I'm afraid . . .
I'll miss it . . .
Yet . . .
Will you still be here by my side?

Untitled

The tides of life have been swept away.
People . . .
Places . . .
Cherished moments . . .
All too quickly.
Busy lives . . .
Task so important . . .
Ultimately they wash away . . .
Like castles in the sand.
Look for the rainbow in the clouds . . .
Beyond your trials and tribulations . . .
Don't let life or words bring you to your knees.

Desperately seeking

November again . . .
The leaves are falling . . .
One more year has come and gone . . .
Everything has changed . . .
I look at the cerulean skies . . .
The grandeur of schemes to come . . .
I'm not invincible like I use to believe . . .
This immense pain I feel . . .
Inside my brain . . .
Day by day, the pain getting stronger . . .
Drowning . . .
Desperately seeking
For
A
Life
Raft . . .

Overwhelmed

Feeling overwhelmed . . .
By everything on my to do list . . .
Like a hamster running on a spinning wheel . . .
But going nowhere . . .
I'm looking for a sanctuary . . .
My brain like a cluttered closet . . .
The need to feel contentment with who I am . . .
What I have accomplished . . .
Serenity . . .
Peace . . .
Tranquility . . .
Tranquility in my mind.

Convoluted dream

Like waterfalls . . .
Tears they cascade down my cheeks . . .
As my life feels like it's reached it's peak.
I need to be taken to a new plateau . . . I can feel the pain of uncertainty . . .
Only I can see . . .
Looking in the mirror . . .
Longing for a reflection to gaze back at me . . .
Telling me I was worth seeing . . .
Wishing the reflection spoke to me . . .
Do I still have time?
Time to make a difference in my own existence?
An epiphany . . .
Dismissed with denial . . .
I feel like I am running and getting nowhere . . .
Like some . . .
Convoluted dream . . .

Shadow of a Dreamer

There is a young girl trapped inside of me . . .
A dreamer . . .
A believer . . .
Somewhere she still lingers.
Dreaming of a life she has fantasized . . .
A life she
has romanticized . . .
Am I delusional?
Am I egotistical?
What am I afraid of?
Always so brave and carefree on the outside . . .
For the world to see . . .
While deep inside . . .
She hides . . .
Living in bondage.
There is a young girl trapped inside of me . . .
Waiting to be set free . . .
A dreamer . . .
A believer . . .
She's but a shadow . . .

"all that we see or seem is but a dream within a dream"
Edgar Allen Poe

Untitled

Melodic gurgles . . .
Contented yawns . . .
Sleepy smiles.
Special moments . . .
Special accomplishments . . .
Go by so quickly . . .
Spontaneous antics caught on camera . . .
Baby sounds of satisfaction . . .
We must capture . . .
In . . .
Our memories . . .
To cherish forever . . .

Untitled

How can life offer so many different things to see and enjoy
Yet . . .
We are wasting our life on pain and regret.
As I look at the glorious mountain ranges
That rise into the heavens . . .
The sky as blue as the crystal ocean.
The pristine lakes that stretch as far as your eyes can see.
It's all within our reach . . .
We hide nestled in our own corner of the past . . .
That has turned into the present.

"Do not go where the road may lead . . . Go instead . . . where there is
no path and leave a trail"
Ralph Waldo Emerson

Cage of silence

Like an animal trapped in a cage . . .
A cage of silence . . .
As my spirit is dying a slow death.
No way out . . .
Responsibilities . . .
Complications . . .
. . . . my world . . .
A jungle . . .
Twisted limbs . . .
Dreary, dark and rainy . . .
Same old dream . . .
The search for inner peace . . .
Unfound . . .
Despair . . .
Loneliness . . .
My world . . .
A cage of silence . . .

Why

Life . . . death . . . suffering . . . redemption
The origin of being . . .
How can such a benevolent god permit needless human suffering . . .
An adventure into our own minds.
The mysterious area between matter and thought.
There is a connection . . .
Between the physical and the intangible.
Abstract question . . .
How do we deal with them???
We incarcerate . . .
Medicate . . .
Educate . . .
Our notions of morality are central to our understandings
Of what makes each of us . . .
An individual . . .

Untitled

Living a masquerade for the world to see . . .
Being held captive by my own fears . . .
I'm sinking in the depth of the ocean . . .
Drowning in my own tears.
Like two bull elephants . . .
Linked in mortal combat . . .
Bellowing . . .
Roaring . . .
Imprecations and abuse . . .
Tearing each other apart.
As we live separate lives within four walls.
A genius . . .
With frailties and problems . . .
And demons to dance with . . .
. . . as we all do . . .

Voice With No Sound

I'm in a hospital . . .
I know it's serious . . .
I'm scared . . .
Am I dreaming???
Someone please wake me up.
I scream . . . yet no sound emerges from me . . .
I feel as if I am floating . . .
No pain . . .
Serene . . .
I see clouds . . .
Blue skies . . .
Suddenly . . .
I feel again . . .
A tube presses my tongue . . .
Flat on the floor of my mouth
As it bulges against my teeth.
A pipe reaches down my throat
Pulling my lips down on that side.
I wake up inside my eyelids . . .
I listen . . .
I see . . .
I cannot speak . . .
NO VOICE . . .
Am I dreaming???
Someone please wake me up . . .
I hear waves . . .
Whooshing . . .
A machine with a rhythm only partially
Related to my own is breathing for me.
It blasts air into my lungs . . .
Before I have a chance to empty them completely.
My body aches for air . . .
I try to signal the doctors, the nurses . . .
I move my finger . . . or so I think I do . . .

Phantomlike.
I wave . . .
My hands tied down . . .
My arms, too weak to move.
I hear the sound outside my room . . .
My FAMILY . . .
They stare at me and speak to me . . .
With such sad eyes . . . bloodshot . . .
. . . crying . . . as they squeeze my hand.
I CAN HEAR YOU . . .
PLEASE DO NOT CRY . . .
I scream . . . yet no sound emerges from me.
Silence . . .
Am I dreaming???
Someone please wake me up . . .
This is not happening to me . . .
I need to sing . . . to dance . . . I have so much
Living to do . . . my family needs me . . .
Suddenly . . . I feel as if I am floating . . . light . . .
No pain . . . serene . . . I see clouds, blue skies . . .
HEAVENS DOOR . . .

"teach us . . . that we may feel the importance"
of every day, of every hour, as it passes."
—from a prayer by Jane Austin

A powerful loss

Losing your connection to the very life that gave you breath . . .
A profound experience . . .
With many repercussions . . .
When both your eyes lock . . .
These eyes will effect your life in a profound way.
They serve a purpose to teach us a lesson.
It may seem horrible and unfair . . .
But in reflection . . .
By overcoming these obstacles . . .
You would have never realized . . .
Your potential strength . . .
Willpower . . .
And heart . . .
The successes . . .
The downfalls . . .
A lesson so important and poignant . . .
The death of a parent . . . A POWERFUL Loss . . .

What we once enjoyed . . . and deeply loved we can never lose.
For all that we love deeply becomes a part of us"
Unknown Author

Synchronicity of Goodbye

My heart screams as I waite for her eyes to open . . .
As they stare into oblivion.
I watch her chest
Rise and fall, hour after hour . . .
In between breaths as the room throbs.
I gently kneel by her bed, as I stare at her . . .
. . . . So INANIMATE . . .
The last vestige of color had been completely
Drained from her face.
I wonder if I will say the right thing . . .
If she even hears me . . .
I want to pour out my heart and soul . . .
My POETRY . . .
But instead . . . My voice frozen in time . . .
At the end of words . . .
Only breathing . . .
As I put my head on her chest
I hear the sound of only my breathing . . .
She is GONE . . .
Silenced in eternal bliss . . .
As I cry to the SYNCRONICITY OF GOODBYE . . .

"and can it be that in a world so full and busy, the loss of one
creature makes a void in any heart so wide and deep, that nothing
but the width and depth of eternity can fill it up"
Charles Dickens

Legend Within

I stare at a photo in a scrapbook . . .
A smile from across the decades . . .
I look into her eyes . . .
I see how she possesses the courage . . .
And strength . . .
Pure intellectual . . .
Passionate . . .
Erudite . . .
That I have always admired.
Then I realize . . .
Part of her . . .
I recognize in myself . . .
She is a legend to me . . .
She has been with me along the way.

A Thread Of Serenity

The natural rhythm of nature
Death . . .
A thread of serenity . . .
Spirituality . . .
As you look down from heaven . . .
My sad face you see, as I cry immensely for your loss.
A difficult passing for those of us you left behind.
Only in my dreams will I find the solace that my soul is searching for.
     . . . A Thread Of Serenity . . .

Untitled

My heart is pounding on my wounded soul . . .
As memories evoked through my own tears.
Tired of living for tomorrow . . .
Part of me still wasn't living for today.
Looking for a diversion . . .
Unrealistic expectations . . .
Impractical . . .
Insatiable . . .
Nothing is perfect . . .
Do I just like the chase?
If I caught the brass ring
Would I try to catch it again?
Alone I sit . . .
Listening . . .
To the silence . . .
Another day . . .
Seeking for salvation . . .
In other places . . .

Untitled

I am being tested . . .
By devastation and tragedy . . .
My life . . .
Full of criticism and fear . . .
Fear of the unknown . . .
The haunting of my inner soul . . .
My being . . .
As I try to live my life . . .
I see the rhapsody of my own shadow . . .
The fears I have kept hidden inside . . .
As sadness fills the void from my anger . . .
I am exhausted . . .
Exhausted . . . from such loss of LIFE . . .

Untitled

Pursuing the ultimate . . .
The ultimate challenge . . .
Anything less than than a total experience . . .
Or a total achievement . . .
Is unacceptable . . .
It . . .
Escapes . . .
Me . . .

Untitled

You make feel perfect and magical . . .
As I look up to the stars so bright . . .
They seem to pour out of the sky like cream from a pitcher . . .
I imagined I was in heaven . . .
A paradise . . .
Another dimension . . .
In sync with the rhythm of the deep blue sea.
You and I . . .

Untitled

It pulls you . . .
As the magic begins . . .
Filled with expectations and promises . . .
The flame that draws the moth . . .
It glows in the warmth of the autumn light.
In the end . . .
The fantasy . . .
Is as fleeting as the fireworks on the fourth . . .

Untitled

The priceless one . . .
Invaluable . . .
The glowing sparkle . . .
Effortless wit . . .
Infinite wisdom . . .
The purity of a child . . .
As they look up to the moon and stars . . .
With . . .
Elated contentment.

Poetry

Words that are written from the depth of my heart and soul . . .
Words that are powerful . . .
They represent all that I was . . .
And all that I am . . .
Without these words I would be lost.
These words are my inner core . . .
They need to be set free . . .
Released . . .
My sanctuary . . .
My escape . . .
They offer refuge when my world is in commotion . . .
My brain sizzling with anticipation.
An antidote . . . from my pain . . .
An empty sheet of paper waiting for words . . .
Like an empty canvas waiting for a splash of color . . .
That is POETRY . . .

"When we take to dream . . .
we discover the many windows to our soul"

Isabella Buroni